1 Introduction

The land area of the United States is large, both in absolute size and in value. Land has long been recognized as a primary input in production and as a store of wealth. Despite its fundamental role in nearly all economic activity, there is no current and complete estimate of the value of the land area of the United States. This paper attempts to begin filling this gap. To fully measure land quantities, prices, and values by sector as recommended by Jorgenson, Landfeld, and Nordhaus (2006) and according to precise System of National Accounts (2008) guidelines would be an enormous undertaking and is not done so here. Rather, the present paper seeks to establish some baseline methods and estimates in hopes of spawning future research on this important topic.

There is a fundamental issue that makes estimation difficult. While farmland quantities and values have been regularly tracked by the U.S. Department of Agriculture (USDA) since the 19th century, urban land is typically transacted as part of a bundle including structures and other improvements, making separated land value data difficult to estimate and tabulate. Because the most valuable land is in cities, the issue of land-structure value separability is fundamental to national land value accounting. A large and growing body of research seeks to disentangle the value of land from structures. This can be loosely grouped in to three main research lines; the "residual" approach of Case (2007), Davis and Heathcote (2007), and Davis (2009), the spatial transactions-based approaches of Haughwout, Orr, and Bedoll (2008), and Nichols, Oliner, and Mulhall (2013), and the hedonic methods of Diewert (2010), and Diewert, de Haan, and Hendriks (2011).

Another issue concerns data availability for the entirety of the land area of the United States. This has resulted in a piecemeal approach to land wealth tabulation, which is inadequate for national accounting purposes. For instance, Case (2007) examines residential vs non-residential (but developed) land, Davis and Heathcote (2007) calculate the value of residential land, and the Office of Management and Budget (2012) estimates the value of federal land. Even Davis (2009), who estimates the value of land by ownership sector with an eye towards national accounting, misses land that is owned by federal, state, and local governments. These limited efforts are likely driven by data availability, as most of this work relies on the Federal Reserve/Bureau of Economic Analysis Flow of Funds Accounts (FFA). Unfortunately, as Davis (2009) notes, the property value measures in the FFAs were not intended to be used for land accounting, and therefore leave out vast areas of land, among other issues.

This paper breaks with the recent tradition of estimating land aggregates using existing property and structure aggregates, and instead proposes a different, micro-based strategy. First, the entirety of the land area of the United States is split into a mosaic of parcels, census tracts, and counties. Then, each piece of land is valued and its legal form of ownership ("sector") is assigned.[1] Estimates of land prices, quantities, and values by sector are then tabulated.[2] In this method, the "quantity" of land is one-dimensional and consisits of its area. All variation in lot desirability is therefore captured by land prices which vary dramatically over space.

In order to apply this method, a variety government and private data sources are employed. The land area of the United States is first divided into Census tracts. By starting with the whole of the geographic area of the country, the micro-based approach proposed in this paper does not omit any land. Each tract is then spatially merged with satellite data on land cover in order to determine shares of each land type, including crops, forests, developed, water, and several others. For land that is undeveloped, farm land values from the U.S. Department of Agriculture's (USDA) Agricultural Census and June Survey are used to estimate land prices. For land in each tract that is developed, hedonic coefficients for land are used to estimate land prices. This has been done by Kuminoff and Pope (2013), and their estimates are used throughout sections of the paper pertaining to developed land. Kuminoff and Pope's (2013) hedonic land price parameters are estimated using real estate listings data including land quantities, home values, and other property and structure attributes, on a sample of tracts. These estimates are taken as given and then interpolated to all remaining tracts using the Census' American Community Survey data. The District of Columbia is treated separately because of its high concentration of federal land. In this area, an assessor's database is used to separate land into various sectors, and land values based on appraisals are tabulated.

The value of the land of the contiguous (lower 48) states is then computed for 2000-2009. From 2000-2006, the value rose 26% from $20.8 trillion to $26.2 trillion, after which, from 2006-2009, it fell 12% to $23.0 trillion. 24% of the land area and 8% of the total value is owned by the Federal government. 6% of the land area is developed, and this land consists

---

[1]For the remainder of the paper, "land" price and value estimates include ecosystems (e.g. root systems such as alfalfa), basic siting improvements (e.g. fencing, irrigation, and land clearing), and stocks of natural resources that convey with the land (e.g. timber, water, hunting, and fishing rights). This approach is not in accordance with System of National Accounts guidelines, but additions/subtractions to the aggregated land value estimates here should be relatively straightforward to compute given that aggregates for various land improvements and stocks of resources already exist.

[2]Ideally, land areas would be at the greatest level of disaggregation–the level of the parcel–because of the high degree of spatial disaggregation and the clarity of ownership. Such a database does not exist. For more information on efforts to construct a national parcel database, see Folger (2011) and HUD (2013).

of 51% of the total value. Agricultural land is 47% of the total land area of the U.S., while consisting of 8% of its total value. Federal land is worth, on average, $4,100 per acre vs $14,600 per acre for non-Federal land. Developed land is worth an average of $106,000 per acre, versus non-developed land, which is estimated to be worth about $6,500 per acre. Agricultural land is estimated to be worth $2,000 per acre vs non-agricultural land which is worth an average of $21,000 per acre.

These estimates are difficult to compare directly to other estimates in the literature because of the different quantities of land considered. For instance, for the year 2005, Davis and Palumbo (2008) estimates household-owned urban land to be worth $9.7 trillion, Case (2007) estimates the total value of land to be $10.8 trillion, excluding government and rural non-farm land, and Davis (2009) estimate the value of non-government land to be about $11 trillion. The estimates in this paper give the total value of land of about $ 25 trillion in the same time period, with $1.8 trillion owned by the Federal government, $13 trillion developed, and $1.1 trillion agriculture. The value for developed in particular is slightly above these existing estimates, but within an admissable distance from prior estimates.

Robustness exercises give some idea of the confidence of the $23 trillion estimate in 2009. Various specifications and samples are used to estimate different land value parameters, with most resulting aggregate tabulations falling between $20 and $25 trillion. The estimates in the paper are therefore generally interpreted as having +/- 10% error.

The remainder of the paper is outlined as follows. First, a broad overview of the literature on land valuation and the estimation framework used in the paper is given. Next, the various data sources used in the estimates are described. Results are then presented and these estimates are compared to past efforts to estimate values of portions of the U.S. land area.[3] The paper then concludes with some potential ways to improve the present analysis.

2   Literature and Estimation Framework

Ideally, every plot of land would be transacted in every period, with prices logged. In this case, land wealth computations would be trivial–all that would be required would be to add up the values of each parcel. Instead, the land market is characterized by two defining attributes: (1), land is often transacted as part of a bundle of goods, including structures; and (2), any individual plot of land (or a bundle including a plot) is not often transacted.

---

[3]Throughout, it should be noted that there are several shortcomings and numerous possibilities for additional research into different aspects of the land valuation methodology presented here, and such efforts are highly encouraged.

When multiplying the low probability that a particular plot of land is transacted in a period with the probability that the plot is vacant, the resulting unconditional probability that an plot is both unimproved and sold in a given period is very low. This requires any calculation of land wealth to consist of mostly estimated values.

To begin, assume the value of a property is the value of land plus structures.

$$V = P^L Q^L + P^S Q^S \tag{1}$$

This decomposition of a property's value into its land and structure components is nearly universal in the literature. The land valuation problem concerns the fact that, while V, Q^S, and Q^L are often observed, P^L and P^S are usually unobserved and must be estimated. For unimproved properties, $Q^S = 0$ so the price per unit of land area is simply the observed property price V divided by the land area Q^L. Beyond this simple case, however, a number of different techniques have been developed to estimate P^L.

Land price estimation in the literature

The first approach is the residual approach, which attempts to exploit the prevalence of data on property values, structure quantities, and structure cost measures. Knowledge of these three variables enables rearranging Equation 1 to give $P^L Q^L = V - P^S Q^S$. The amount $P^L Q^L$ is then attributed to the value of the land. This approach is favored by Case (2007) and Davis (2009) because aggregate property value and aggregate value of structures series exist in the Federal Reserve Board/Bureau Economic Analysis Flow of Funds tables, making land value calculations using this method relatively straightforward. The major issue with this approach is that the value of structures series is calculated using the replacement cost of structures while assuming that the replacement value is a good estimate of the market value. This assumption is violated in declining areas such as the industrial Midwest where the asset value of homes is often far less than replacement costs, and in booms or busts in the national housing market, where structures are priced differently than the replacement cost would suggest.[4] Consequently, there are times when the land value is negative when estimated in this manner, such as for the Corporate Business sector in 2009 (see Bureau Economic Analysis, 2013), or with unreasonably high growth rates (89% between 1985Q2 and 1985Q3 for Massachusettes) such as those found in Davis and Palumbo (2008).

---

[4]See Glaeser and Gyourko (2005) for good discussion of the implications of urban decline on structure values.

The second approach is the spatial transactions-based approach recently developed in papers such as Haughwout, Orr, and Bedoll (2008), and Nichols, Oliner, and Mulhall (2013). This approach uses vacant land and/or tear-down sales to set $Q^S = 0$ in Equation 1, allowing land prices to be calculated as $P^L = V/Q^L$. This approach is ideal in locations with large numbers of land-only sales or when structuers are sparse and a relatively small component of the total property value. Unfortunately, the number of land transactions falls substantially in downturns in the housing market, and land-only sales near city-centers where values are the highest are often infrequent. Methods have been developed to deal with each of these issues, but the data requirements of the approach are steep and the assumptions can become problematic in downturns and in large cities.

The third approach considered here is the hedonic approach. This method begins with the base equation $V = P^L Q^L + P^S Q^S$ and estimates P^L and P^S over a cross-section or panel of transactions. This traditional implicit price estimation technique has the advantage that all property transactions that include land can be used to estimate price parameters, making the selection and sparse data problems less of an issue, and allowing for prices in more heavily disaggregated geographic areas to be estimated. There is a wide literature on various hedonic techniques, as well as documentation of various advantages and problems. One of the most relevant is the finding of Diewert (2010), that structure and land prices are correlated, making it potentially problematic to try to disentangle the two in practice. In order to address this issue, Diewert (2010) places parameter restrictions on structure prices similar to the residual approach, allowing land prices to vary freely. Kuminoff and Pope (2013) rely on the large number of observations in each sample to mitigate the variance consequences of collinearity.

Estimation framework for developed land

Each of the three prior methods in the literature have their associated benefits and costs: the residual approach has low data requirements but somewhat unreliable estimates in downturns; the spatial transactions-based models are potentially more accurate, but have substantial data requirements and suffer from some selection issues; and finally, the hedonic approach is perhaps less accurate than the spatial transactions-based models, but has data requirements that are substantially easier to meet. Given the need for land price estimation over a large number of highly disaggregated land areas, and the increasing prevalence of local-area hedonic land price estimates using real estate listings data, this approach is used to estimate land prices for developed land.

Kuminoff and Pope (2013) produce one such set of hedonic land price estimates, and these are well-suited to the problem at hand. Their price estimates are at the census tract level over a cross-section of cities from 2000-2009. The strategy in this section is to extrapolate these land prices to all areas in the United States with developed land using Census data. This approach gives a reasonable panel of land prices over time.

Hedonic land price estimates from Kuminoff and Pope (2013)

Kuminoff and Pope (2013) employ a dataset of real estate transactions from across the United States to construct land prices per unit of land area for census tracts in ten MSAs. The specification below is estimated for each MSA i, in census tract j, for property k at time t,

$$\ln V_{ijkt} = \zeta_{ijt} + \delta_{ijt} \ln Q_{ijkt}^L + \gamma_{ijt} \ln sqft_{ijkt} + x_{ijkt}'\beta_{it} + \varepsilon_{ijkt} \tag{2}$$

This parameterization assumes the fixed effect, the price of land per unit of area, and the price of the structure per unit of interior space, all vary by census tract and time period, but that structure attribute prices are constant within a city for a given time period.[5] The value of land for a particular property is then calculated as $\hat{V}_{ijkt}^L = \hat{\zeta}_{it} + \hat{\delta}_{ijt}Q_{ijkt}^L$, and the average land price per acre in the census tract is computed as

$$\hat{P}_{ijt}^L = \frac{1}{N_{ijt}} \sum \frac{\hat{V}_{ijkt}^L}{Q_{ijkt}^L} \tag{3}$$

This procedure is conducted by Kuminoff and Pope (2013) for 2,978 of the 72,150 tracts in the lower 48 United States (in 2009; other years vary slightly), and their land price estimates are employed throughout the remainder of the paper.

Interpolating land prices to the rest of the U.S.

Having acquired a panel of land prices by census tract for each time period, the question now turns to the estimation of land prices in tracts that Kuminoff and Pope (2013) do not estimate. Absent valid instruments or identifying restrictions, a reduced-form model under long-run assumptions is the best model available when it is necessary to incorporate every

---

[5]Diewert (2010) evaluates a number of different hedonic methods, including that which is performed by Kuminoff and Pope (2013). While Diewert finds greater accuracy using hedonic models where value is additive in structure and land attributes instead of multiplicative, and those with quality-adjusting structure attributes using the age of the dwelling, empirically, he finds that most hedonic methods give similar results.

populated census tract in the U.S. into the interpolation.[6] The form of this interpolation is given motivation by rearranging Equation 1 such that $P^L = (V - P^S Q^S)/Q^L$. Each included variable represents one of these right-hand-side arguments with parameters having the same predicted signs.

The following model contains the following right-hand-side variables, and these data exist for every populated census tract in the U.S.: residential home value, number of rooms, population density, and the median age of the housing stock.[7] Value corresponds to V, so α_1 is predicted to be positive, *ex ante*, The number of rooms correspond to Q^S, so $\alpha_2 < 0$. Because tracts have a relatively fixed population by definition, higher density is associated with lower Q^L, meaning $\alpha_3 > 0$. Finally, the median age of the housing unit gives a negative structure quality adjustment (Q^S) because of depreciation, with a resulting larger land share of value, giving $\alpha_4 > 0$.

$$\hat{P}^L_{ijt} = \alpha_{0t} + \alpha_{1t} value_{ijt} + \alpha_{2t} rooms_{ijt} + \alpha_{3t} density_{ijt} + \alpha_{4t} age_{ijt} + \epsilon_{ijt} \qquad (4)$$

Under the (admittedly very strong) assumption that tracts are at their steady-states and the correlations between the left- and right-hand side variables are similar both in and out of sample, Equation 4 gives estimates of the value of residential land when structures are present for each census tract in the U.S for each time period. Following estimates by Albouy and Ehrlich (2012) that suggest residential land values are nearly equivalent to overall land values, the estimated residential land values can be reasonably assumed to be equal to other developed land values.

Table 1 shows the results of this model estimated for each year from 2000-2009. Parameter estimates are fairly stable, suggesting a small degree of estimation error because these are independent draws from the same sample of tracts. The one major exception is median value, with estimated α_{1t} rising from about 0.85 in the early years up to about 1.10 in the later ones. Were this a structural model, this parameter non-constancy would be a major cause for concern. However, because of the reduced-form, interpolatory nature of the exercise, the signs and the R^2 values are the most important. All signs are consistent with predictions and each model explains over 2/3 of the variation in land prices, indicating a very high fit for a cross-sectional model. This is reflected in Figure 2, which shows the land price on the

---

[6]When the census tract is unpopulated, this interpolation of urban land is not used. Instead, land value tabulations are based on agricultural land values.

[7]It would be desirable to include a construction cost index for P^S, but due to the reliance on within-city variation for parameter estimation, and the fact that construction cost indices are usually at the city level (including R.S. Means), this variable is omitted.

vertical axis with the most predictive right-hand-side variable, median house prices.

There are several concerns with this approach that should be noted. First, there is the question of the generalizability of the Kuminoff and Pope (2013) sample of cities, which are at the larger end of the U.S.' city size distribution. It is implicitly assumed that the within-city variation in land value shares can be applied to cities not in the sample. Because the cities in the estimation sample are larger than the average, with presumably higher land values, it is possible that this approach results in a bias when extrapolated to the rest of the sample. For this reason, robustness tests are conducted using several other samples and specifications, such as the inclusion of a $value^2$ term on the right-hand side of the equation, MSA-specific fixed effects, a "Rust Belt" only sample, and a "high growth" city only sample. Aggregate values are robust to reasonable model alterations, but are of questionable sample robustness. The implications of these different approaches on land value calculations are considered in Section 4.

Estimation framework for undeveloped land

In contrast to developed land, excellent data on agricultural land prices are available and computed annually by the Department of Agriculture. The largest issue regarding land pricing then becomes the wide tracts of land that have never been transacted, such as land that was never claimed during the United States' homesteading period and is now public domain land administered by the Forest Service and the Bureau of Land Management. This land, by virtue of its unclaimed status, is likely inferior to claimed land in both observable and unobservable characteristics. A model that can help explain the observed variation in agricultural land values is developed here in order eliminate the observed heterogeneity. Unobservable heterogeneity is likely to still exist and has the potential to cause problems, but it is likely small in absolute terms due to the low presumed value of land that is both inferior and unclaimed.

A standard hedonic model can be applied to questions of rural land valuation much in the same manner as urban land valuation (see Torrell, 2005, for example). Important factors include the land type, ecosystems existing on the land, and of particular importance, the area's level of urbanization, which reflects both transportation costs and the development option value of the land (see Guiling, Brorsen, Doye, 2009). A simple model able to uncover the implicit values of the development option as well as land characteristics over time is given in the following model, where i, j, and t index the county, state, and time period, respectively, α is a state-level fixed effect, X is a vector of land ecosystem types, and $urban$ is a variable

9

measuring the "urbanness" of the county in terms of its population and proximity to other population centers.

$$V_{ijt} = \alpha_{jt} + X'_{ijt}\beta_{jt} + \gamma_{jt}urban_{ijt} + \epsilon_{ijt} \tag{5}$$

This model is estimated using observed agricultural land prices and characteristics. Land prices for Federal land are then interpolated based on these estimated hedonic coefficients and observed characteristics.

3 Data

The data used to apply the methods in the prior section of estimating both urban and rural land prices are from a variety of public and private sources. These data include real estate listings data, satellite imagery, Census Bureau and Department of Agriculture surveys and tabulations, the General Service Administration's Federal Real Property Profile database, tax assessment data, and several GIS shapefiles.

National Land Cover Database

The National Land Cover Database (NLCD) consists of coded satellite imagery with a resolution of 30m × 30m. This dataset is produced by the United States Geological Survey every five years. The most recent release is 2006. For more information see Homer et al. (2004) and Fry et al. (2011). The NLCD is a raster with 16 different land cover classifications, following the Anderson Land Cover Classification System (Anderson, 1976). For an example of the information in the NLCD, see Figure 1 for land classifications around the White Sands Missile Range in New Mexico. This figure shows the center region which is barren due to missile testing, along with areas of development (shades of red), grassland, and scrubland (yellow-brown), and forest (green). The exceptional resolution of this database allows for accurate tabulations of land types at small levels of geography.

National Atlas

The National Atlas is a division within the Department of the Interior. It produces GIS shapefiles of different maps, including a map of all Federal and Indian lands with an area greater than 640 acres (1 square mile). A spatial union of a U.S. county map with the map of Federal and Indian lands produces a map with U.S. counties divided into non-Federal land and Federal land by administering agency.

The National Atlas map on Federal lands is best used for large, rural land plots. While items such as naval bases and national monuments appear reasonably defined in the data, even for urban areas, the file misses smaller parcels. This necessitates the use of the Federal Real Property Profile database of smaller parcels owned by the federal government.

Federal Real Property Profile

The Federal Real Property Profile (FRPP) is a database created by the General Services Administration (GSA) in accordance with Executive Order 13327 of February, 2004. This includes all land and buildings that are owned or leased by the Federal Government, with the exception of public domain land and national parks and wildlife refuges. The FRPP includes information on 34,126 parcels. Because the National Atlas includes all land areas greater than 1 square mile (640 acres), all properties with a land area of 600 acres or greater are omitted. At this threshold, duplication between the data sources is minimal without erroneously dropping unique parcels in the FRPP database. This filter leaves 32,447 parcels totaling 1,401,798 acres (2,190 sq. mi.). This database misses agencies not subject to appropriation such as the Federal Reserve Board and the Securities and Exchange Commission, but is close to the universe of all small federally held properties.

Tax assessor data

Washington, DC has a publicly available parcel database with separate tax assessments for land and structures. Many parcel databases exist for other areas as well, but the time cost of fully implementing a parcel-based approach is cost-prohibitive.[8] Because of the prevalence of federally owned parcels in the District, and the superiority of this source compared to the Federal Real Property Profile, which misses certain parcels owned by the U.S. government, the DC parcel database is the employed in this area. There are certainly issues with appraisals, including documented biases in agricultural land appraisals according to Ma and Swinton (2012). Additionally, appraisals may have other idiosyncrasies that cause estimates to depart from true values, such timing lags between appraisals or the methods of the land value appraisals themselves, which must be estimated. Urban land that is not subject to taxation also may have biases because the tension in the desire for high versus low appraisals from the assessor versus the property owner paying taxes does not exist.

---

[8]The cost and feasibility of a national parcel database has been investigated by Folger (2011) and U.S. Department of Housing and Urban Development, Office of Policy Development and Research (2013).

Ownership in the District is established by the owner name of the property. A sequence of key words such as "United States of America," "Forest Service," "National Park Service" and others are used as search phrases against the parcel database, with properties matching the name attributed to the Federal government. In the District of Columbia parcel database, 2,727 of the 136,459 parcels are owned by the Federal government as of 2012, for a total of 7,279 acres, compared to 4,470 acres in the FRPP and National Atlas. Therefore, it is crucial, at least in the District, to use a parcel database to calculate a reasonable value of federal land.

USDA Census of Agriculture and June Survey

The Census of Agriculture is performed every five years by NASS, and measures farm prices by farm land type by county. This data provides useful information on undeveloped land prices over space. While the Census of Agriculture is every five years, there also exists an annual survey at the state level, called the June Area Survey, also produced by NASS. This survey contains land prices by crop land type. Using the Census county-level variation in prices, along with the June Area Survey's state-level land prices in each year, it is possible to calculate land value by crop land type for each year in each county. The disaggregated NASS agricultural land values are constructed net of large improvements such as structures, but may include improvements such as fences, wells, grading, and biological capital such as orchards or alfalfa root systems. These non-structure improvements confound the land values, and further work should account for this fact.

American Community Survey

The American Community Survey is an annual survey of households performed by the Census Bureau. This survey includes information on demographics, housing units, commuting, and other socioeconomic indicators. Summary data are publicly available at the Census tract level using a 5-year rolling sample. Census tracts are geographic areas that are meant to be relatively stable over time, and consist of 1,000 to 8,000 people, with an ideal size of 4,000. Because information exists on all census tracts, this is the ideal dataset for interpolation of a representative sample of areas to the entirety of the United States.

Hedonic Land Value Estimates from Real Estate Listings Data

Land value estimates are based on hedonic models in Kuminoff and Pope (2013). Kuminoff and Pope (2013) use data on single-family home sales to estimate the hedonic model in Equation 2 which allows the construction of census tract-specific land price measures that are then interpolated to other areas. These data include common listings variables, including the interior square feet, the lot square feet, the number of bathrooms, bedrooms, the age of the dwelling, and others. The sample of areas in Kuminoff and Pope (2013) is likely not representative of the nation as a whole. However, due to the large number of census tracts (over 3,000) in the cities, within-city variation perhaps makes the estimates satisfactorily generalizable for the following reason: Bertaud and Brueckner (2005) suggest that the edges of cities are all quite similar, so edge-tracts of any city may be similar to edge tracts in every other city, and therefore every city has at least some tracts represented in the sample.

Putting it all together

Stitching these data sources together to derive meaningful land value estimates begins with a map of the United States' census tracts. The next step is to perform a spatial union with the National Atlas shapefile which categorizes land into that which is known to be federally owned and that which may not be. These are defined as "Atlas" versus "non-Atlas" areas. Raster pixel counts of land cover from the National Land Cover Database are then tabulated for each area in this shapefile. Federal Real Property Profile parcels are then assigned to the federal side of the ledger with characteristics equivalent to the non-Atlas parcels. This sequence of operations gives tabulated land area by land cover type by census tract by federal/non-federal ownership. American Community Survey data and the Kuminoff and Pope (2013) land price estimates are then merged onto this tabulation at the census tract level, USDA Census of Agriculture data at the county level, and the USDA June Survey at the state level.

Each county has two available land prices, one for developed and one for undeveloped land. The choice of price shares to use for each parcel is based on the share of developed land in the National Land Cover Database. If a county has no population, the undeveloped price is used for the entire area. If a county has no agricultural land, the developed price is used for the entire area.

4   Results

The methods in the prior section are applied from 2000-2009, which is the time over which hedonic estimates exist in Kuminoff and Pope (2013). Overall results are encouraging, as they follow the general trends in land prices expected over the decade. Figure 3 shows that from 2000-2006, the value rose 26% from $20.1 trillion to $26.2 trillion, after which, from 2006-2009, it fell 12% to $22.9 trillion. Figure 6 shows the spatial distribution of land value per acre (land "prices"). This figure shows higher land prices in the east, west, and midwest regions; population centers; and forested areas of the Rocky Mountains.

As Table 3 indicates, of the 1.89 billion acres in the lower 48 states, 24% of the land area and 8% of the value is owned by the federal government, and 6% of the area and 51% of the value is consists of developed land. Agricultural land is 47% of the total land area of the U.S., while consisting of 8% of its total value. These shares do not sum to one because they are not mutually exclusive. For instance the Federal government owns a large amount of developed and agricultural land. Federal land is worth, on average, $4,100 per acre vs $14,600 per acre for non-Federal land. Developed land is worth an average of $106,000 per acre, versus non-developed land, which is estimated to be worth about $6,500 per acre. Agricultural land is estimated to be worth $2,000 per acre vs non-agricultural land which is worth an average of $21,000 per acre.

This table also shows that, within states, a great deal of variation is seen in land acres, land value, and the quantity and value of both federal and developed land. California is the most valuable state by a large margin, worth approximately $3.9 trillion in 2009. The lowest average land value is Wyoming, with 62 million acres worth about $90 billion. 87% of the land area of Nevada is owned by the federal government, but this land is only worth 45% of the land value in the state due to the fact that much of the federal land is undeveloped pasture. The most developed "state" is the District of Columbia, with 87% of its land area covered by roads or buildings. Rhode Island and New Jersey are both 31% developed. Several states have just 1% developed land, including Wyoming, New Mexico, Montana, and Nevada. There are 6 states with over 80% agriculture land: Oklahoma, Iowa, Kansas, North and South Dakota, and Nebraska. The states with under 10% of their land dedicated to agriculture are the District of Columbia, Maine, Nevada, and New Hampshire.

Table 4 gives how much a particular state represents of the total area and value amounts. 60% of all federal land is concentrated in 7 states: Nevada (12%), California (10%), Arizona (10%), Montana (7%), Idaho (7%), and Utah (7%), and New Mexico (7%). The value of federal land is much more evenly distributed. While California makes up 18% of the nation's federal land holdings in value terms, most other states with large land quantities are those with lower land prices. For example, Wyoming has 7% of federal land acres, but only 2.9% of the value, whereas the sum of Massachusetts, D.C., and Maryland have the same value in only 0.06% of federally held land area. Texas has the highest quantiy of developed land with 9.8% of the U.S. total. However, California, with 6% of the developed land area, has 26% of all developed land value, compared to Texas' 4.5% of the national total.

Potential Biases and Comparison with Past Estimates

It is important address the possibility of bias and estimation error at this point. Estimation error is likely relatively small, as evidenced by the fact that the annual values are estimated independently and the results seem sensible and do not fluctuate dramatically from year to years. However, there is a real possibility of several sources of economically meaningful bias in the estimates.

One source of bias considers improvements to land. Both rural agricultural land and urban developed land often have substantial improvements that are inseparable from the land and are thus purchased in a bundle that includes the land. This is impossible to remove using the approach in this paper, and may be significant in value terms. In order for land valuation to follow Commission of the European Communities, International Monetary Fund, Organisation for Economic Cooperation and Development, United Nations and World Bank (2008) guidelines in more formal accounting efforts, improvements must be tabulated and valued separately. As it stands, the land value is biased in a positive direction due to this effect.

In general the biases all seem to be positive. This suggests that the estimates presented in this paper are likcly higher than would be estimated after properly accounting for improvements and given a more representative estimation sample. This is reinforced when viewed in the light of past land value estimates. In general, past estimates shown in Table 6 suggest that the total land value of residential land was about $8 to $10 trillion in 2005, with the total value of non-government land of $11 to $13 trillion. Additionally, the Office of Management and Budget (OMB) produces estimates of Federal land values, with recent estimates of around $0.4 to $0.5 trillion. In the OMB case, this only considers rural land. However, the other estimates seem at least on the order of magnitude of the estimates presented in this paper, while being somewhat lower. Therefore, the true value is likely somewhat lower than those presented in this paper.

5 Conclusion

This paper presents new estimates of the value of land in the lower 48 United States from 2000 to 2009. In 2009, the value of land was approximately \$23 trillion, \$1.8 billion of which is owned by the federal government. According to the National Land Cover Database, 6% of the lower 48 states is developed, and according to the estimates in this paper, this land consists of 50% of the overall land value. Land values rose until 2006 and then fell until the end of the sample in 2009.

The estimation methodology consists of dividing the U.S. into a mosaic of parcels at the census tract level and below, assigning ownership and prices to each parcel, and tabulating. Whereas past estimates have omitted large areas of land or have based valuation on potentially implausible estimates of structure values, this attempt instead misses no land area and uses hedonic estimates of land values.

While there are potentially some shortcomings with this approach as it is currently implemented, as parcel data become more widespread and consolidated, these shortcomings will diminish. For instance, in the District of Columbia parcel data, it is possible to divide land area by ownership sector according to Commission of the European Communities, International Monetary Fund, Organisation for Economic Cooperation and Development, United Nations and World Bank (2008) guidelines, and along with appraised land values, quickly and easily tabulate a rudimentary land wealth account. With more sophisticated methods such as the sales-price, appraisal ratio (SPAR) method of Bourassa et al. (2006), it may be possible to refine the methodology outlined in this paper into a true land wealth account for the United States.

References

Albouy, D. and Ehrlich, G. (2012). Metropolitan land values and housing productivity. Working Paper 18110, National Bureau of Economic Research.

Anderson, J. R. (1976). *A land use and land cover classification system for use with remote sensor data*, volume 964. US Government Printing Office.

Bertaud, A. and Brueckner, J. K. (2005). Analyzing building-height restrictions: predicted impacts and welfare costs. *Regional Science and Urban Economics*, 35(2):109–125.

Bourassa, S. C., Hoesli, M., and Sun, J. (2006). A simple alternative house price index method. *Journal of Housing Economics*, 15(1):80 – 97.

Bureau of Economic Analysis (2013). Relation of BEA's Current-Cost Net Stock of Private Structures to the corresponding items in the Federal Reserve Board's Financial Accounts of the United States. url: http://www.bea.gov/national/pdf/st13.pdf.

Case, K. E. (2007). The value of land in the United States: 1975-2000. In *Proceedings of the 2006 Land Policy Conference: Land Policies and Their Outcomes*, pages 127–147. Lincoln Institute of Land Policy Press.

Commission of the European Communities, International Monetary Fund, Organisation for Economic Cooperation and Development, United Nations and World Bank (2008). *System of National Accounts, 2008*. United Nations.

Davis, M. A. (2009). The price and quantity of land by legal form of organization in the United States. *Regional Science and Urban Economics*, 39(3):350–359.

Davis, M. A. and Heathcote, J. (2007). The price and quantity of residential land in the united states. *Journal of Monetary Economics*, 54(8):2595–2620.

Davis, M. A. and Palumbo, M. G. (2008). The price of residential land in large U.S. cities. *Journal of Urban Economics*, 63(1):352–384.

Diewert, W. E. (2010). Alternative approaches to measuring house price inflation. Technical report, Discussion Paper 10-10, Department of Economics, The University of British Columbia.

Diewert, W. E., de Haan, J., and Hendriks, R. (2011). The Decomposition of a House Price Index into Land and Structures Components: A Hedonic Regression Approach. *The Valuation Journal*, 6(1):58–105.

Folger, P. (2011). Issues regarding a national land parcel database. *Congressional Research Service*.

Fry, J., Xian, G., Jin, S., Dewitz, J., Homer, C., Yang, L., Barnes, C., Herold, N., and Wickham, J. (2011). Completion of the 2006 national land cover database for the conterminous united states. *PERS*, 77(9):858–864.

Glaeser, E. L. and Gyourko, J. (2005). Urban decline and durable housing. *Journal of Political Economy*, 113(2):345–375.

Guiling, P., Brorsen, B. W., and Doye, D. (2009). Effect of urban proximity on agricultural land values. *Land Economics*, 85(2):252–264.

Haughwout, A., Orr, J., and Bedoll, D. (2008). The price of land in the New York metropolitan area. *Federal Reserve Bank of New York: Current Issues in Economics and Finance*, 14(3).

Homer, C., Huang, C., Yang, L., Wylie, B., and Coan, M. (2004). Development of a 2001 national land-cover database for the United States. *Photogrammetric Engineering and Remote Sensing*, 70(7):829–840.

Jorgenson, D. W., Landefeld, J. S., and Nordhaus, W. D. (2006). *A new architecture for the US national accounts*, volume 66. University of Chicago Press.

Kuminoff, N. V. and Pope, J. C. (2013). The value of residential land and structures during the great housing boom and bust. *Land Economics*, 89(1):1–29.

Ma, S. and Swinton, S. M. (2012). Hedonic valuation of farmland using sale prices versus appraised values. *Land Economics*, 88(1):1–15.

Nichols, J. B., Oliner, S. D., and Mulhall, M. R. (2013). Swings in commercial and residential land prices in the United States. *Journal of Urban Economics*, 73(1):57 – 76.

Office of Management and Budget (2012). *Fiscal Year 2013: Analytical Perspectives*. U.S. Government Printing Office.

Torell, L. A., Rimbey, N. R., Ramirez, O. A., and McCollum, D. W. (2005). Income earning potential versus consumptive amenities in determining ranchland values. *Journal of Agricultural and Resource Economics*, pages 537–560.

U.S. Department of Housing and Urban Development, Office of Policy Development and Research (2013). The feasibility of developing a national parcel database: County data records project final report. Technical report.

Figure 1: White Sands Missile Range, NM, Land Cover, 2006

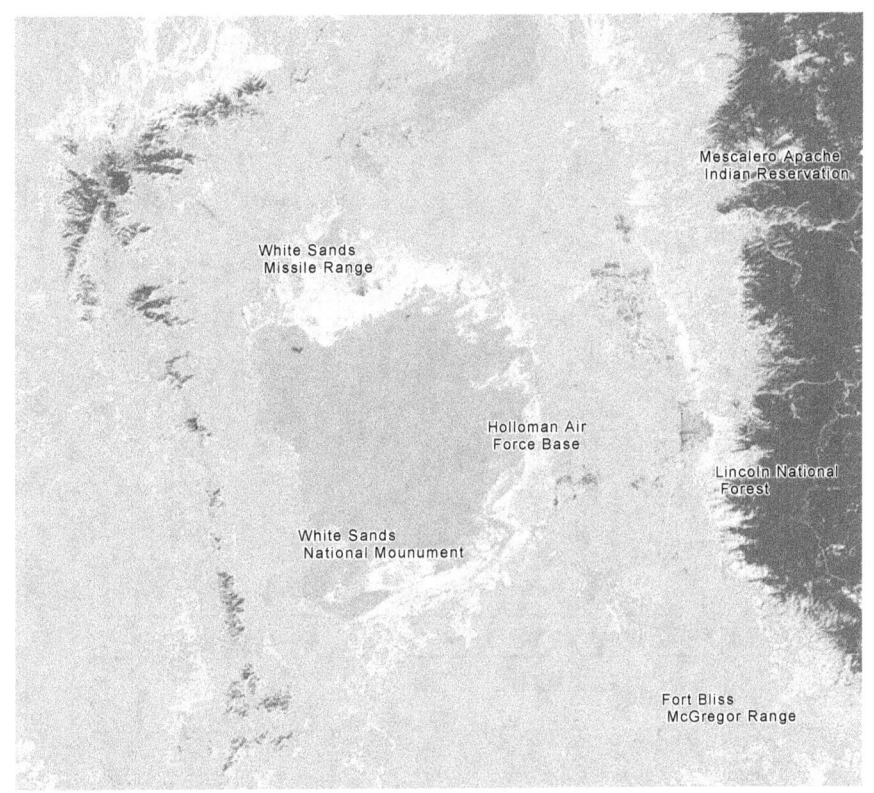

Figure 2: Results of Land Value Interpolation from Kuminoff and Pope (2013) using Census (ACS) data, 2009

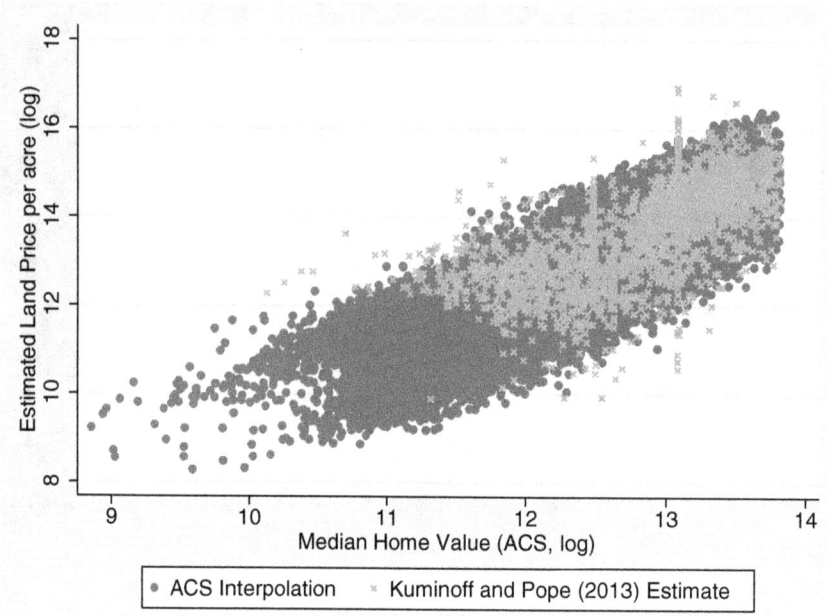

Figure 3: Land Value of the Lower 48 States, 2000-2009

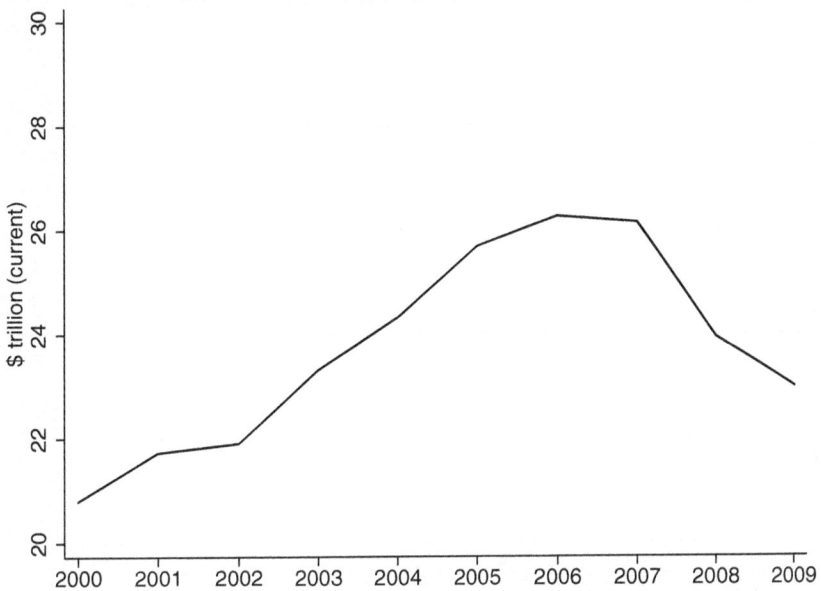

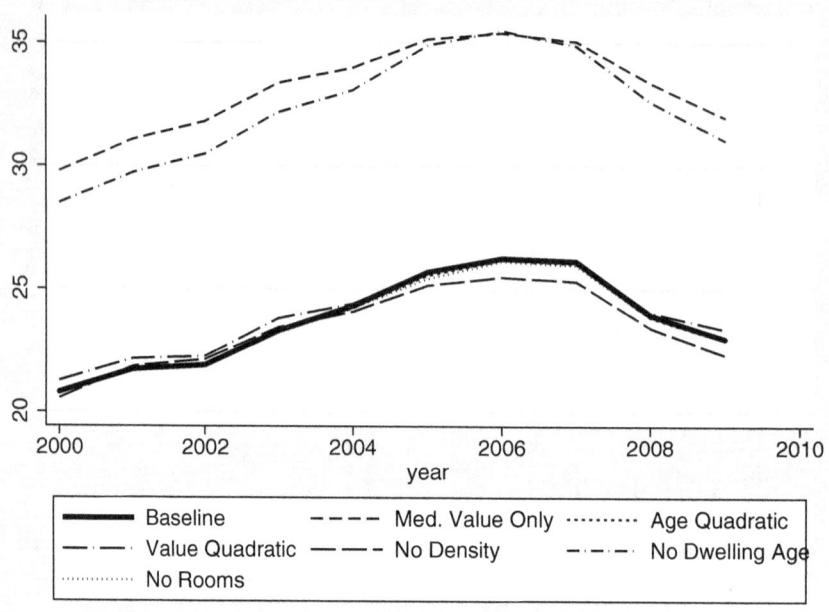

Figure 5: Land Value of the Lower 48 States, 2000-2009, Sample Robustness

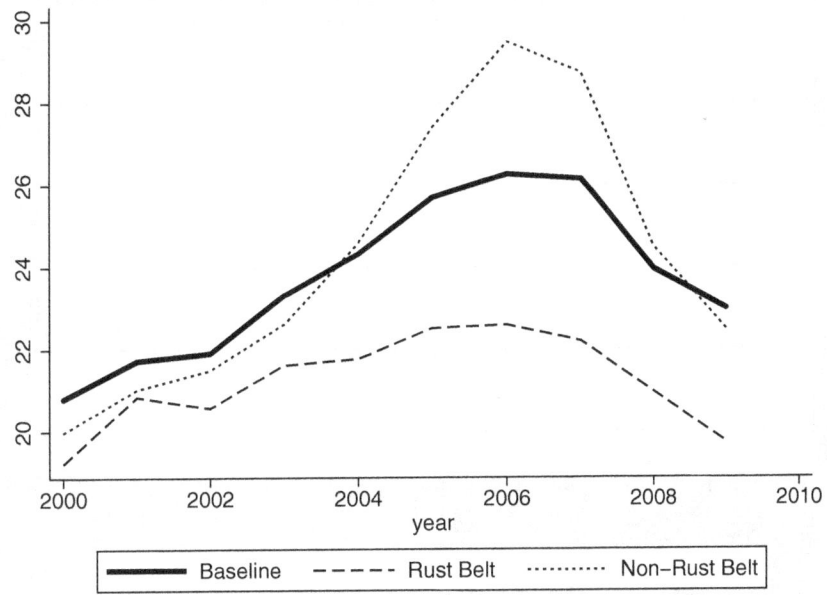

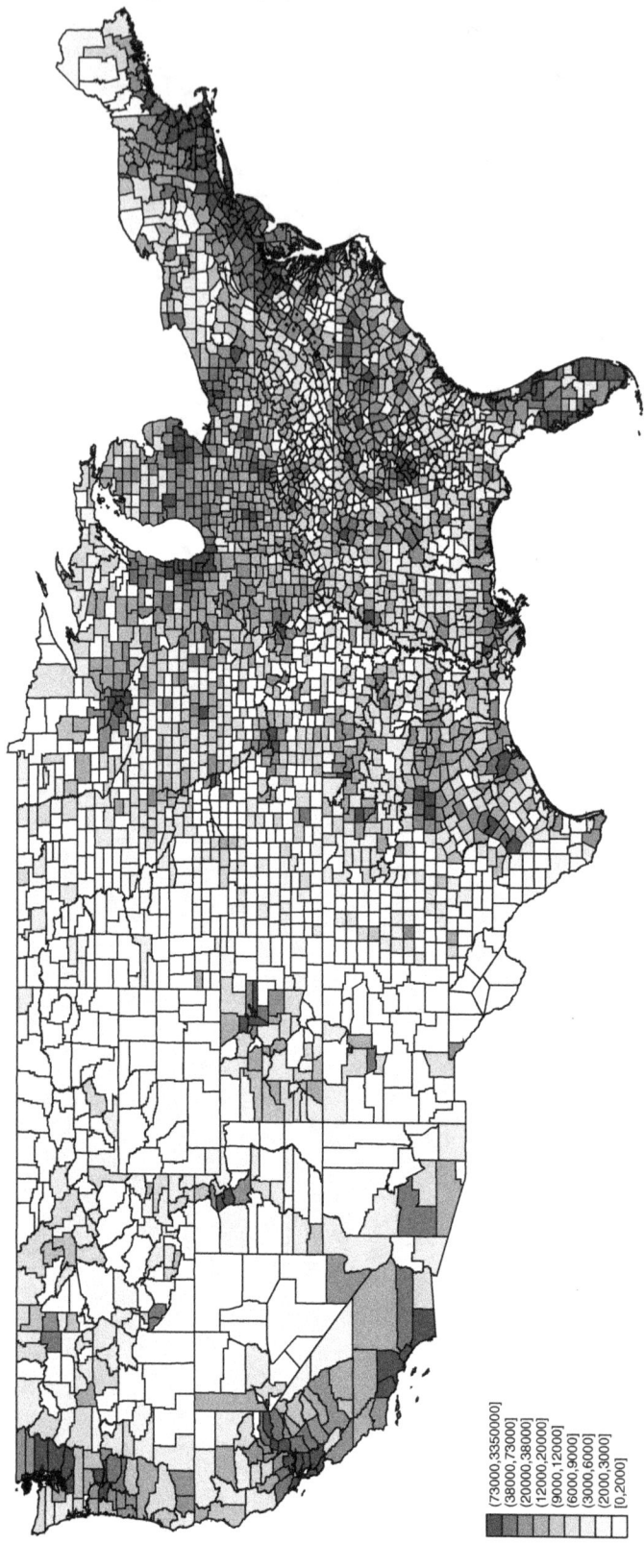

Figure 6: Land Price per Acre in the Lower 48 States, 2009

Table 1: Land price interpolation estimates

Dependent variable: Land Price per Acre (log)

Year	2000	2001	2002	2003	2004	2005	2006	2007	2008	2009
Property Value	0.908***	0.905***	0.942***	0.930***	1.048***	1.099***	1.121***	1.095***	1.125***	1.164***
	(0.0210)	(0.0206)	(0.0201)	(0.0193)	(0.0192)	(0.0193)	(0.0199)	(0.0202)	(0.0211)	(0.0226)
Rooms	-0.148***	-0.162***	-0.171***	-0.175***	-0.202***	-0.220***	-0.244***	-0.219***	-0.183***	-0.177***
	(0.0150)	(0.0147)	(0.0143)	(0.0137)	(0.0137)	(0.0138)	(0.0142)	(0.0144)	(0.0150)	(0.0161)
Tract Density	0.303***	0.283***	0.293***	0.294***	0.310***	0.323***	0.344***	0.333***	0.289***	0.284***
	(0.0158)	(0.0155)	(0.0151)	(0.0145)	(0.0145)	(0.0145)	(0.0150)	(0.0152)	(0.0159)	(0.0170)
Age of Housing Unit	0.375***	0.357***	0.336***	0.348***	0.297***	0.272***	0.183***	0.261***	0.346***	0.435***
	(0.0373)	(0.0367)	(0.0356)	(0.0342)	(0.0341)	(0.0343)	(0.0354)	(0.0359)	(0.0374)	(0.0401)
Constant	0.692**	1.033***	0.755**	1.004***	-0.0511	-0.406	-0.210	-0.326	-1.366***	-2.301***
	(0.311)	(0.306)	(0.297)	(0.286)	(0.285)	(0.286)	(0.295)	(0.300)	(0.312)	(0.335)
Observations	1,917	1,917	1,918	1,919	1,919	1,917	1,917	1,919	1,917	1,916
R-squared	0.659	0.660	0.686	0.703	0.739	0.755	0.752	0.738	0.715	0.699

Notes: Standard errors in parentheses. *** $p < 0.01$, ** $p < 0.05$, * $p < 0.1$. Property Value, Rooms, and Age of Housing Unit are medians; Property Value, Tract Density, and Age of Housing Unit are in logs. The table presents reduced-form models of land prices. Models are estimated separately for each year.

Table 2: Land Quantities and Values by Sector: Washington, DC, 2013

	Acres	Value	P/Acre
Households and NPISH	14,431	$ 26,691,233,792	$ 1,849,604
Non-Financial, Non-Corporate Business	5,019	$ 33,426,939,179	$ 6,660,575
Non-Financial, Corporate Business	2,985	$ 9,667,046,481	$ 3,238,784
Financial Business	249	$ 1,823,793,668	$ 7,315,267
State and Local Government	2,578	$ 8,029,715,968	$ 3,114,669
Federal Government	7,279	$ 29,549,412,352	$ 4,059,712
Total	32,540	$ 109,188,141,440	$ 3,355,482

Table 3: Land Quantities and Values in the Lower 48 States, 2009

State	Area (000s acres)	Value ($millions)	Federal Area	Federal Value	Developed Area	Developed Value	Agriculture Area	Agriculture Value
Alabama	32,374	400	4.8%	6.0%	7.0%	27.3%	27.9%	5.1%
Arizona	72,778	315	43.1%	24.3%	2.2%	55.3%	19.8%	6.8%
Arkansas	33,238	224	12.2%	12.6%	5.9%	18.4%	41.6%	15.5%
California	99,893	3,905	51.8%	8.4%	6.8%	78.4%	24.7%	4.6%
Colorado	66,387	429	39.8%	31.8%	2.8%	38.7%	46.8%	7.5%
Connecticut	3,105	400	0.1%	0.3%	24.7%	61.5%	13.1%	1.2%
Delaware	1,248	72	2.0%	1.3%	17.5%	46.1%	40.9%	6.1%
Dist. Of Columbia	40	42	18.4%	20.1%	87.3%	82.6%	0.0%	0.0%
Florida	35,254	1,021	12.1%	3.7%	14.8%	65.8%	25.5%	4.8%
Georgia	37,074	528	8.0%	5.4%	9.6%	38.4%	27.2%	5.6%
Idaho	52,988	182	65.0%	49.8%	1.7%	16.8%	21.7%	11.0%
Illinois	35,459	833	3.0%	2.0%	12.0%	58.8%	75.5%	13.7%
Indiana	22,896	387	3.9%	3.4%	10.8%	35.0%	64.5%	15.1%
Iowa	35,661	235	0.3%	0.5%	7.5%	25.4%	86.2%	50.7%
Kansas	52,131	220	0.9%	2.8%	5.2%	32.8%	88.8%	20.2%
Kentucky	25,385	183	9.7%	2.8%	7.4%	32.1%	55.1%	21.3%
Louisiana	27,424	354	6.2%	6.5%	7.6%	35.4%	29.4%	4.8%
Maine	19,863	122	0.9%	4.1%	3.6%	22.4%	6.8%	2.3%
Maryland	6,231	470	2.7%	5.1%	18.0%	55.4%	32.5%	2.7%
Massachusetts	5,058	517	2.0%	3.9%	25.6%	61.6%	10.1%	1.2%
Michigan	36,398	865	14.5%	3.6%	10.8%	45.7%	27.6%	3.9%
Minnesota	50,788	416	8.1%	6.4%	5.7%	45.6%	53.0%	17.7%
Mississippi	29,831	166	8.9%	6.8%	6.3%	27.3%	38.3%	13.1%
Missouri	43,967	318	7.6%	3.7%	6.9%	39.5%	66.0%	20.2%
Montana	93,312	213	31.1%	44.2%	1.4%	8.8%	65.2%	18.8%
Nebraska	49,054	144	1.6%	2.2%	3.6%	26.0%	92.7%	42.9%
Nevada	70,427	149	86.8%	44.6%	1.0%	48.7%	7.4%	2.5%
New Hampshire	5,746	114	14.4%	2.1%	8.0%	34.5%	8.2%	2.0%
New Jersey	4,735	930	3.4%	2.0%	30.7%	68.6%	15.4%	1.1%
New Mexico	77,679	150	37.0%	25.9%	1.2%	29.7%	46.3%	10.1%
New York	30,135	1,245	0.8%	1.1%	9.4%	66.2%	23.8%	1.4%
North Carolina	31,176	506	12.9%	5.3%	10.4%	35.7%	27.1%	6.7%
North Dakota	43,696	110	6.5%	7.5%	4.1%	13.2%	90.7%	33.4%
Ohio	26,125	838	3.7%	2.4%	14.7%	42.5%	53.4%	6.2%
Oklahoma	43,865	323	3.4%	5.4%	6.1%	24.5%	79.9%	13.6%
Oregon	61,514	400	54.9%	28.9%	2.7%	36.6%	26.5%	8.1%
Pennsylvania	28,631	914	3.0%	1.3%	12.1%	41.3%	27.3%	4.2%
Rhode Island	673	90	0.7%	2.7%	31.4%	69.6%	9.7%	1.2%
South Carolina	19,250	339	9.4%	5.4%	9.1%	26.8%	25.4%	4.2%
South Dakota	48,235	103	8.5%	13.4%	2.9%	10.5%	90.5%	44.1%
Tennessee	26,368	380	8.1%	7.2%	9.2%	33.7%	41.6%	9.9%
Texas	167,859	1,266	2.6%	4.5%	6.4%	41.5%	74.2%	14.7%
Utah	52,964	247	68.8%	42.9%	1.7%	31.7%	20.4%	5.8%
Vermont	5,915	44	11.3%	11.7%	5.5%	16.3%	20.8%	8.3%
Virginia	25,318	555	15.2%	9.6%	9.5%	48.8%	31.9%	6.0%
Washington	42,742	716	31.3%	13.0%	6.0%	53.6%	32.4%	4.5%
West Virginia	15,375	162	13.0%	3.6%	7.0%	17.4%	24.0%	5.7%
Wisconsin	34,662	344	6.3%	2.6%	7.4%	42.8%	43.7%	14.7%
Wyoming	62,266	97	50.2%	54.1%	0.9%	10.9%	48.5%	16.9%
Lower 48 Total	1,893,194	22,982	23.6%	8.0%	5.8%	50.7%	47.0%	8.0%

27

Notes: The table presents estimates of quantities and values of all land area in the lower 48
United States plus the District of Columbia for 2009. Federal shares are calculated using
National Atlas and Federal Real Property Profile databases. Developed shares are calculated
based on land cover (developed includes categories 21, 22, 23, and 24 on the USGS' modified

Table 4: State Land Quantity and Value Shares of Total, 2009

State	All		Federal		Developed		Agricultural	
	Land	Value	Land	Value	Land	Value	Land	Value
Alabama	1.7%	1.7%	0.3%	1.3%	2.1%	0.9%	1.0%	1.1%
Arizona	3.8%	1.4%	7.0%	4.2%	1.5%	1.5%	1.6%	1.2%
Arkansas	1.8%	1.0%	0.9%	1.5%	1.8%	0.4%	1.6%	1.9%
California	5.3%	17.0%	11.6%	17.9%	6.2%	26.3%	2.8%	9.8%
Colorado	3.5%	1.9%	5.9%	7.4%	1.7%	1.4%	3.5%	1.8%
Connecticut	0.2%	1.7%	0.0%	0.1%	0.7%	2.1%	0.0%	0.3%
Delaware	0.1%	0.3%	0.0%	0.0%	0.2%	0.3%	0.1%	0.2%
District Of Columbia	0.0%	0.2%	0.0%	0.5%	0.0%	0.3%	0.0%	0.0%
Florida	1.9%	4.4%	1.0%	2.1%	4.8%	5.8%	1.0%	2.7%
Georgia	2.0%	2.3%	0.7%	1.6%	3.3%	1.7%	1.1%	1.6%
Idaho	2.8%	0.8%	7.7%	4.9%	0.8%	0.3%	1.3%	1.1%
Illinois	1.9%	3.6%	0.2%	0.9%	3.9%	4.2%	3.0%	6.2%
Indiana	1.2%	1.7%	0.2%	0.7%	2.3%	1.2%	1.7%	3.2%
Iowa	1.9%	1.0%	0.0%	0.1%	2.5%	0.5%	3.5%	6.5%
Kansas	2.8%	1.0%	0.1%	0.3%	2.5%	0.6%	5.2%	2.4%
Kentucky	1.3%	0.8%	0.5%	0.3%	1.7%	0.5%	1.6%	2.1%
Louisiana	1.4%	1.5%	0.4%	1.2%	1.9%	1.1%	0.9%	0.9%
Maine	1.0%	0.5%	0.0%	0.3%	0.7%	0.2%	0.2%	0.2%
Maryland	0.3%	2.0%	0.0%	1.3%	1.0%	2.2%	0.2%	0.7%
Massachusetts	0.3%	2.2%	0.0%	1.1%	1.2%	2.7%	0.1%	0.4%
Michigan	1.9%	3.8%	1.2%	1.7%	3.6%	3.4%	1.1%	1.9%
Minnesota	2.7%	1.8%	0.9%	1.5%	2.7%	1.6%	3.0%	4.0%
Mississippi	1.6%	0.7%	0.6%	0.6%	1.7%	0.4%	1.3%	1.2%
Missouri	2.3%	1.4%	0.8%	0.6%	2.8%	1.1%	3.3%	3.5%
Montana	4.9%	0.9%	6.5%	5.1%	1.2%	0.2%	6.8%	2.2%
Nebraska	2.6%	0.6%	0.2%	0.2%	1.6%	0.3%	5.1%	3.4%
Nevada	3.7%	0.6%	13.7%	3.6%	0.6%	0.6%	0.6%	0.2%
New Hampshire	0.3%	0.5%	0.2%	0.1%	0.4%	0.3%	0.1%	0.1%
New Jersey	0.3%	4.0%	0.0%	1.0%	1.3%	5.5%	0.1%	0.5%
New Mexico	4.1%	0.7%	6.4%	2.1%	0.8%	0.4%	4.0%	0.8%
New York	1.6%	5.4%	0.1%	0.8%	2.6%	7.1%	0.8%	1.0%
North Carolina	1.6%	2.2%	0.9%	1.5%	3.0%	1.6%	0.9%	1.9%
North Dakota	2.3%	0.5%	0.6%	0.4%	1.6%	0.1%	4.4%	2.0%
Ohio	1.4%	3.6%	0.2%	1.1%	3.5%	3.1%	1.6%	2.8%
Oklahoma	2.3%	1.4%	0.3%	0.9%	2.4%	0.7%	3.9%	2.4%
Oregon	3.2%	1.7%	7.6%	6.3%	1.5%	1.3%	1.8%	1.8%
Pennsylvania	1.5%	4.0%	0.2%	0.6%	3.2%	3.2%	0.9%	2.1%
Rhode Island	0.0%	0.4%	0.0%	0.1%	0.2%	0.5%	0.0%	0.1%
South Carolina	1.0%	1.5%	0.4%	1.0%	1.6%	0.8%	0.5%	0.8%
South Dakota	2.5%	0.4%	0.9%	0.7%	1.3%	0.1%	4.9%	2.5%
Tennessee	1.4%	1.7%	0.5%	1.5%	2.2%	1.1%	1.2%	2.0%
Texas	8.9%	5.5%	1.0%	3.1%	9.8%	4.5%	14.0%	10.1%
Utah	2.8%	1.1%	8.2%	5.8%	0.8%	0.7%	1.2%	0.8%
Vermont	0.3%	0.2%	0.1%	0.3%	0.3%	0.1%	0.1%	0.2%
Virginia	1.3%	2.4%	0.9%	2.9%	2.2%	2.3%	0.9%	1.8%
Washington	2.3%	3.1%	3.0%	5.1%	2.3%	3.3%	1.6%	1.8%
West Virginia	0.8%	0.7%	0.4%	0.3%	1.0%	0.2%	0.4%	0.5%
Wisconsin	1.8%	1.5%	0.5%	0.5%	2.4%	1.3%	1.7%	2.7%
Wyoming	3.3%	0.4%	7.0%	2.9%	0.5%	0.1%	3.4%	0.9%

Notes: The table presents estimates of quantities and values of all land area in the lower 48 United States plus the District of Columbia for 2009. Federal shares are calculated using National Atlas and Federal Real Property Profile databases. Developed shares are calculated based on land cover (developed includes categories 21, 22, 23, and 24 on the USGS' modified Anderson scale). Agricultural shares are calculated based on the USDA's agricultural census and June surveys. Shares in rows do not sum to 1 because shares are not mutually exclusive.

Table 5: State Land Quantity and Value Shares of Total, 2009

Urban Influence Code	Definition	Land Area (million acres)	Land Value ($millions)	Average Value ($/acre)	Federal Land	Federal Value	Developed Land	Developed Value
1	In large metro area of 1+ million residents	181	$ 11,733	$ 64,844	21%	4%	17%	71%
2	In small metro area of less than 1 million residents	424	$ 7,015	$ 16,558	21%	9%	8%	41%
3	Micropolitan area adjacent to large metro area	71	$ 476	$ 6,681	26%	9%	6%	18%
4	Noncore adjacent to large metro area	65	$ 303	$ 4,677	20%	9%	5%	7%
5	Micropolitan area adjacent to small metro area	155	$ 718	$ 4,628	22%	13%	5%	14%
6	Noncore adjacent to small metro area and contains a town of at least 2,500 residents	201	$ 705	$ 3,501	20%	17%	4%	6%
7	Noncore adjacent to small metro area and does not contain a town of at least 2,500 residents	82	$ 215	$ 2,625	18%	20%	3%	4%
8	Micropolitan area not adjacent to a metro area	212	$ 736	$ 3,473	32%	22%	3%	12%
9	Noncore adjacent to micro area and contains a town of at least 2,500 residents	112	$ 312	$ 2,794	24%	19%	3%	6%
10	Noncore adjacent to micro area and does not contain a town of at least 2,500 residents	115	$ 264	$ 2,291	25%	25%	3%	4%
11	Noncore not adjacent to metro or micro area and contains a town of at least 2,500 residents	140	$ 281	$ 2,007	33%	28%	2%	6%
12	Noncore not adjacent to metro or micro area and does not contain a town of at least 2,500 residents	136	$ 224	$ 1,655	23%	28%	2%	3%

Notes: The table presents estimates of quantities and values of all land area in the lower 48 United States plus the Dist. of Columbia for 2009. Federal shares are calculated using National Atlas and Federal Real Property Profile databases. Developed shares are calculated based on land cover (developed includes categories 21, 22, 23, and 24 on the USGS' modified Anderson scale).

Table 6: Previous U.S. Land Value Estimates

Author	Sector	Finding	Year
Case (2007)	Residential Land	$9.5tr	2005
Case (2007)	Non-residential Land*	$1.3tr	2005
Davis and Heathcote (2007)	Residential Land (non-farm)	$5.0tr	2005
Davis (2009)	Households and NPISH	$7.6tr	2005
Davis (2009)	Nonfinancial, Noncorporate Business	$2.2tr	2005
Davis (2009)	Nonfinancial, Corporate Business	$0.8tr	2005
Davis (2009)	Financial Business	$0.1tr	2005
Census of Agriculture	Farm Land**	$1.7tr	2007
Office of Management and Budget (2012)	Federal Land	$0.4tr	2010

Notes:

* Excludes government land and rural, non-farm land

** Includes buildings